What Is Perseverance of the Saints?

Basics of the Reformed Faith

How Do We Glorify God?
How Our Children Come to Faith
What Are Election and Predestination?
What Is Biblical Preaching?
What Is a Reformed Church?
What Is a True Calvinist?
What Is Justification by Faith Alone?
What Is Perseverance of the Saints?
What Is Providence?
What Is Spiritual Warfare?
What Is the Christian Worldview?
What Is the Lord's Supper?
What Is True Conversion?
Why Do We Baptize Infants?

What Is Perseverance of the Saints?

Michael A. Milton

P&R PUBLISHING
P.O. BOX 817 • PHILLIPSBURG • NEW JERSEY 08865-0817

Unless otherwise indicated, Scripture quotations are from The Holy Bible, English Standard Version, copyright © 2001 by Crossway Bibles, a division of Good News Publishers. Used by permission. All rights reserved.

Italics within Scripture quotations indicate emphasis added.

Page design by Tobias Design

Printed in the United States of America

Library of Congress Cataloging-in-Publication Data

Milton, Michael A. (Michael Anthony), 1958–
  What is perseverance of the saints? / Michael A. Milton.
     p. cm. — (Basics of the reformed faith)
  Includes bibliographical references.
  ISBN 978-1-59638-094-3 (pbk.)
  1. Perseverance (Theology) I. Title.
  BT768.M55 2009
  234—dc22

                          2008045550

What is the perseverance of the saints? Can a believer be given the gift of faith and then lose it? Can one be saved by the shed blood of Jesus Christ and then fall away into atheism or agnosticism? Is it possible for a Christian to fall from grace? What about the hard passages which seem to indicate that this is possible? What about the passages that urge Christians to stay true to the end? What about the real cases we know—people who sat beside us in the pew one Sunday but left and rejected Jesus the next? Can we be married to the Savior and choose to divorce God?

The answers to these questions are essential to understanding the Reformed faith. And for those of us who believe, with the famous Baptist preacher Charles Haddon Spurgeon, that the Reformed faith is simply the gospel of Jesus Christ,[1] we would quickly add that the answers are vital to understanding biblical Christianity. As a pastor, I know, through countless firsthand experiences, that these questions and their corresponding answers have a direct correlation with the Christian life. All theology is practical. All truth has an impact on life. This is what Jesus meant when He said that "You will know the truth and the truth will set you free" (John 8:32). There is a resultant freedom that is associated with a deeper understanding of and willful ascent to the Word of God—a sunlit wide and open field of new life that can heal emotions, remove the stain of guilt, and give hope for living and a glorious, holy, defiant, Christ-honoring "blessed assurance" in the face of the tomb.

But I don't want to rush to conclusions. I want to slow down and, if you could imagine it, take a seat beside you. This is not a debate. There are places for that. And I am not going to be "taking on" those who differ. Rather, "To the Law and to the testimony" (Isa. 8:20 KJV) and then "let every man be fully persuaded in his own mind" (Rom. 14:5 KJV). And I also promise that there will be no fighting. "Fighting among believers over doctrine?" you say. Strange but true. I remember when I was a ten-year-old boy at a little country school in South Louisiana. Out on the playground, during one particular recess, I, a little fellow from a Southern Baptist church, got into an argument with a little chap who was from the local Methodist congregation. And our argument was over this very thing: if having been saved by Christ, can you "lose you salvation?" The little Methodist boy (devoutly following Mr. Wesley's line with admirable zeal) said it was possible to be saved and then to lose it, for the Bible said there were those who were a part of the church who fell away. I responded with perfect party talking points, "No way! Once saved, always saved!" I didn't bother to actually answer his claims from the Bible. But our schoolyard debate got heated. In fact there was more heat than light. Disputations from the fifteenth century had nothing on us! We ended up fighting on the playground and had to be broken up by our teacher (who was also my Sunday school teacher). When she learned what we were arguing about she looked perplexed. Or maybe "really ticked off" is a better way of describing her demeanor at that moment! She told us: "You argue about the things of God and then fight each other like little heathens! Now what does that say about the both of you?" Well, it said a lot. And we were both punished as we should have been.

So, no debating, no bashing, and no fighting. Promise.

I assume that you who are reading these words now are in a new members or inquirers' class at a local Presbyterian or Reformed congregation, or you may be traveling on a spiritual journey, digging deeper into the Reformed faith, or possibly even seeking answers to the deeper questions of Scripture. Perhaps you are a prodigal child trying to find your way home. You don't need a lecture or a theological tome on this doctrine to get you there. But you just might like to have a friend—a friend who can relate to you; a friend who once asked, perhaps, the same questions you are asking today about the perseverance of the saints; and maybe even a pastor to open up God's Word for you to discover what we mean when we speak of God's people who are truly His persevering to all eternity. If so, I am your man. Or at least I want to be. So, if you will, pull up a chair. This isn't going to be too long, but I hope—I pray—my words will lead you to discover what I believe is one of the most comforting, gracious and beautiful parts of faith in Jesus Christ according to the Scriptures. Indeed,

I believe that the biblical revelation of the perseverance of the saints "... is a doctrine which lies at the foundation of all the hope which the believer enjoys; it inspires confidence in danger, comfort in sorrow, succor in temptation, and is an 'anchor to his soul' amidst tempests the most violent."[2] I believe the doctrine of the perseverance of the saints is God's gift to us, "the truth" that will "set you free," given in His Word in order to cultivate greater love for God and deeper gratitude to Jesus Christ for His sacrifice on the cross. I believe that this doctrine, like all doctrines, is a faith for living that will lead you to glorify God and enjoy Him forever.

To understand this biblical truth that has shaped so much of Presbyterian and Reformed Christians' faith, we might begin by considering several different aspects of this doctrine:

(1) *A definition of the doctrine*, in which we will see how Scripture answers our questions; (2) *distortions of the doctrine*, in which we will admit that there are popular misconceptions about perseverance of the saints; (3) *a defense of the doctrine* from the Word of God, in which we will admit the difficult passages and seek to interact with them; and finally (4) *delight in the doctrine* and joy in our souls as we meditate together on the practical benefits of this doctrine. I will then offer some closing thoughts on common questions surrounding the doctrine.

One note. As I write to you, I will use endnotes, not only as a reference point, but to illustrate my statements with the very Word of God on this vital topic to your soul. So don't stop without reading the endnotes! Go to them and where I have provided Scripture, study it, soak in it, go back to it, deal with it, pray over it, and inwardly digest it. I have no need to argue this case. I would rather let the fullness of Scripture, attended by the Author of that Scripture, convince you, as He did me.

What then is the truth about the doctrine of the perseverance of the saints?

THE DOCTRINE OF PERSEVERANCE DEFINED

Perseverance Defined Biblically

The truth, which we call the perseverance of the saints, is not an obscure doctrine. One cannot read the Bible without finding evidences of "what God starts, God completes." If one were to go to only one passage in Scripture, as I was challenged to do in my own Christian experience, this one would bring you face to face with this comforting truth:

> My sheep listen to my voice; I know them, and they follow me. I give them eternal life, and they shall never perish; no one can snatch them out of my hand. My Father, who has given them to me, is greater than all; no one can snatch them out of my Father's hand. (John 10:27–29 NIV)

Jesus' metaphor of a shepherd holding lambs provides a warm and pastoral image of the truth that Christ Himself, who saved me, would take responsibility to guard me from eternal harm. No enemy can touch these lambs. But there is more. Here I saw that I heard the voice of Jesus because He knew me. I followed Him because He called me. And because of His initiating work of salvation in my life, I could never perish. I could never fall away completely from my Savior. In fact, as I continued to read in this way, I came to see that I was, in fact, a gift from God the Father to God the Son. And if I were a gift to the Son, in some eternity-past covenant between Father and Son, then the Father was personally involved with my life. He knew my name.[3] I would later hear the singer-songwriter Buddy Greene sing words that led me again to this passage and this truth:

> I'm His gift from the Father, I'm elect by His decree.
> I've chosen to be married to the One who first chose me.[4]

Sovereignty, surety, safety. But this is only one passage. Another passage that God used in my own life was Philippians 1:6. In Philippians, Paul wrote a letter to a congregation that had helped his ministry. So Paul wrote a great epistle of joy. And he also gave these Christians a great gift: the gift of a truth that could set them free. He wrote:

> Being confident of this, that he who began a good work in you will carry it on to completion until the day of Christ Jesus. (Phil. 1:6 NIV)

I was a prodigal son. I had heard the gospel from my Aunt Eva who reared me, and yet in my search for answers to my questions, healing for my pain, and solutions for my situation, and through my heartache as an orphan, my own sinful heart, the sins of my flesh, the temptations of the devil and the world, I "fell away" from the things of God. But I came to see, through the unfathomable grace of God, that when He begins a good work of salvation in our lives, He *will* carry it on all the way to the day of Christ—the very end of time. *I will persevere.* What a great gift this was for me. I was encouraged that even in my waywardness, Christ was there. And what a great gift it is for you this day!

Of all of the Scriptures teaching us about God's keeping power, none is more helpful for the whole study of perseverance of the saints than 1 John 2:19:

> They went out from us, but they were not of us; for if they had been of us, they would have continued with us. But they went out, that it might become plain that they all are not of us.

Here the apostle John not only affirms that true believers among them would have "continued" or persevered, but that there are those who are among the visible church who are not true believers. And they will not persevere. Thus, from this and the many other citations in God's Word, the Reformed faith admits that there are those who fall away, but those who are truly in Christ will continue, though they, too, may fall away for a season.

These are only a few Scriptures. But the doctrine is everywhere upon the pages of Holy Writ. The doctrine is taught explicitly[5] and it is taught implicitly.[6] It is announced in the Old Testament[7] and it is sung in the Psalms;[8] it is taught by our Lord Himself,[9] and it is preached with compassion and excitement by the writers of the New Testament. Consider just a few passages:

> For the gifts and the calling of God are irrevocable. (Rom. 11:29)

> But the Lord is faithful, and he will strengthen and protect you from the evil one. (2 Thess. 3:3 NIV)

> And do not grieve the Holy Spirit of God, *with whom you were sealed for the day of redemption."* (Eph. 4:30, NIV, emphasis added)

> No temptation has overtaken you that is not common to man. God is faithful, and he will not let you be tempted beyond your ability, but with the temptation he will also provide the way of escape, that you may be able to endure it. (1 Cor. 10:13)

> Knowing that he who raised the Lord Jesus will raise us also with Jesus and bring us with you into his presence. (2 Cor. 4:14)

> For this slight momentary affliction is preparing for us an eternal weight of glory beyond all comparison. (2 Cor. 4:17)

> . . . But I am not ashamed, for I know whom I have believed, and I am convinced that he is able to guard until that Day what has been entrusted to me. (2 Tim. 1:12)

The Lord will rescue me from every evil deed and bring me safely into his heavenly kingdom. To him be the glory forever and ever. Amen. (2 Tim. 4:18)

But the Lord is faithful. He will establish you and guard you against the evil one. (2 Thess. 3:3)

Blessed be the God and Father of our Lord Jesus Christ! According to his great mercy, he has caused us to be born again to a living hope through the resurrection of Jesus Christ from the dead, to an inheritance that is imperishable, undefiled, and unfading, kept in heaven for you, who by God's power are being guarded through faith for a salvation ready to be revealed in the last time. (1 Peter 1:3–5)

These passages are only a few priceless gems among the weighty treasure store of scriptural jewels that sparkle with this radiant doctrine. As I read them and prayed over them in my own life, I came to agree with the simple, clear, and radically biblical assessment of the great teacher of the Reformed faith, John Murray:

Those united to Christ by the effectual call of the Father and indwelt by the Holy Spirit, will persevere unto the end.[10]

Perseverance Defined Theologically

Moving from the biblical texts to the interpretation of these passages in the church, one thing is clear: the doctrine of the perseverance of the saints is certainly not new or novel or tangential to the Christian faith. Indeed, except for certain periods in the church, and in particular strands within the church, this truth has been a hallmark of biblical Christianity. As William Cunningham put it,

> This doctrine of perseverance is manifestly a necessary part of the general scheme of Christian doctrine.[11]

As Loraine Boettner wrote in his magisterial book, *Predestination*:

> The great majority of the creeds of historic Christendom have set forth the doctrines of Election, Predestination, and final Perseverance, as will readily be seen by any one who will make even a cursory study of the subject.[12]

Though we hold that the Old Testament prophets taught it, and the psalmist sang of it, and Jesus Christ taught it and Paul and Peter taught it, it is given its first great definition, in post-apostolic church history, by the great church father Augustine. He gives it in the course of a debate with a theological rival, Pelagius, who argued that man could be saved and lose his salvation. Augustine thus wrote (in 428 or 429):

> [The grace of God] which both begins a man's faith and which enables it to persevere unto the end is not given in respect of our merits, but is given ac-

cording to His own most secret and at the same time most righteous, wise, and beneficent will; since those whom He predestinated, them He also called, with that calling of which it is said, "The gifts and calling of God are without repentance."[13]

As John Jefferson Davis summarized the famed church father's position,

> It is clear for Augustine, based on his understand-ing of the Pauline texts in Romans, that God's elect will certainly persevere to the end and attain eter-nal salvation.[14]

If God decreed your salvation from before the foun-dation of the earth, and sent His only begotten Son to live the life you could never live, die a substitutionary death on the cross to pay for your sins, go to the grave and back again, ascend into heaven where He ever prays for you, and the Holy Spirit then graciously came into your life and opened your heart to believe and thus you become a child of God—and all of that was initiated by a lovingly unre-lenting Creator—can all of that ever be undone? Ever?

A word on perseverance and theology and the Bible: Not all words or phrases used to define doctrine are found in the Bible (e.g., "Trinity"). And this is so for "the perse-verance of the saints" (although the famous phrase was employed by the translators of the New American Stan-dard Bible for their translation of the Greek in Revelation 14:12, where we read the divine admonition for the saints to resist aligning themselves with the ungodly powers of this world: "Here is the perseverance of the saints who keep the commandments of God and their faith in Jesus").

But whether it appears in the Bible in word or in carefully collected and sorted revelation, the perseverance of the saints, like all true theology, must be—and is—grounded completely in God's Word, which we have seen. But I believe that the force of all of those Scriptures is summed up in one good biblical word: *grace.* Thus the perseverance of the saints is thoroughly and wondrously grounded in God's grace. Grace is God doing for us what we could not do for ourselves. God created the worlds. He created man in His image. Through sin entering the human race, men were cast into sin. But God made a promise, in Genesis 3:15, that He would redeem mankind from their fallen condition through a "seed" of the woman. This promise is further developed in biblical revelation as God makes a "covenant"[15]—a sacred agreement, a "bond in blood sovereignly administered"[16]—that God would do for us what we cannot do for ourselves: deal with our sin and bring a holiness in which we can be fully restored to God as His sons and daughters. He did this through the life and death and resurrection of Jesus of Nazareth who was and is God in the flesh. The purpose of this book will not allow us to fully explore the scriptural evidences and practical blessings of the Covenant of Grace, but we must, at least, say that the perseverance of the saints, like all other truths related to God's plan of salvation, is grounded in this blessed agreement that God made with man. We can't say everything but we must say this:

- God's grace is grounded in God's love;
- God's grace is centered in God's Son, Jesus Christ;
- God's grace brings faith to repent and believe in God's Son;
- God's grace makes those who believe God's very own children;
- God's grace produces a growing, practical faith in His children that seeks God's glory; *and if all of that is true—and it is!—then it follows, in Scripture, that . . .*
- God's grace will never let us go.

Let's look at it another way.

The doctrine of the perseverance of the saints, the fifth point in the "Five Points of Calvinism,"[17]—or, *The Doctrines of Grace*—logically works out the truth that if God started it, God will complete it. Following the acrostic TULIP we see the logical progression. If man is a sinner (T-*Total Depravity*), and God chooses us not on our merits but completely out of His love (U-*Unconditional Election*), and Christ was sent to die for those whom the Father set His love upon (L-*Limited—or better put, "Particular"—Atonement*), and if He drew them by His Holy Spirit (I-*Irresistible Grace*), then it follows that our salvation is not about us; it is about the love of God, the grace of God, and the purposes of God at work in us. Thus, those whom He set His love on from all eternity are His and He will never let them go. Those for whom Jesus Christ shed His precious blood will never be cut off from Him. Those who have been saved by grace will be kept in His grace—"P": *Perseverance of the Saints.*

But this doctrine also means that through the ordinary means of grace—Word, sacrament, and prayer—believers may face every sort of physical, circumstantial, and spiritual adversity and affliction, and yet, because of the work of the Holy Spirit in them, and because of the seed of faith in them, they will always persevere. They may fall away, Peter-like, from following their Lord for a season, but if they are truly born again by the Spirit of God, they will return to their Father. They will persevere. Or, we may put it better and say, "God will persevere through them." The Dutch theologian Louis Berkhof summed it up like this:

> Perseverance may be defined as that continuous operation of the Holy Spirit in the believer, by which the work of divine grace that is begun in the heart, is continued and brought to completion.[18]

The Westminster Confession of Faith simply says:

> They, whom God has accepted in His Beloved, effectually called, and sanctified by His Spirit, can neither totally nor finally fall away from the state of grace, but shall certainly persevere therein to the end, and be eternally saved. (WCF 17.1)[19]

The prodigious Methodist hymnist Fanny Crosby[20] composed a beautiful, little spiritual song whose title says it all for me: "Safe in the Arms of Jesus":

Safe in the arms of Jesus,
safe on His gentle breast;
There by His love o'ershaded,
sweetly my soul shall rest.[21]

And biblically, theologically, personally, this is what perseverance of the saints means for you.

THE DISTORTIONS OF THE DOCTRINE OF PERSEVERANCE

There are misunderstandings about this doctrine that perhaps result from our own failure to teach the Word as we ought to. Or perhaps the Baptist and the Methodist boy scrapping in the schoolyard have been fighting it out without listening to the heartbeat of the Word. For that there should be repentance. And where I have produced more heat than light, I hope others will forgive me. But look: there are some things that the doctrine is not saying.

The perseverance of the saints is not merely "once saved, always saved." I used this popular phrase rather ineffectively (not to mention un-Christianly) in my schoolyard scuffle. But to be honest the phrase doesn't tell the whole story of the biblical doctrine. "Perseverance" is much preferable. For if we only focus on "once saved, always saved"—without taking anything away from that statement *as is*—we only speak of the believer's *position* in Christ. It does not address the believer's *progression* in holiness, which is sanctification.[22] And that is important because Calvinism is not fatalism. The Reformed faith holds that God is sovereign and man is responsible. The mystery of those two revelations cannot be reconciled except through faith and then obedience to the Lord's commands arising out of that heart of faith. Thus, if I have been called of God and have responded and been given the gift of the Holy Spirit then I will be eager to make my calling and election sure, as Peter admonished:

> Therefore, brothers, be all the more diligent to make your calling and election sure, for if you practice these qualities you will never fall. (2 Peter 1:10)

When he made that famous proof text defending the perseverance of the saints as something which the believer, through faith and works, "cooperates" with, he follows with a strong statement that gives the verse sharp context (in v. 11):

> For in this way there will be richly provided for you an entrance into the eternal kingdom of our Lord and Savior Jesus Christ. (2 Peter 1:11)

Thus, it is not just that we are positionally saved once and for all, but it is that the believer's position is worked out with "fear and trembling"[23] through faith and good works. The examples of David, of Solomon, and of Peter provide living demonstrations of how we who believe that "what God starts, God completes" must also believe that it will happen as we obediently seek Christ and His kingdom before all other things in life.

Thus eternal security comes through a justification that is followed with sanctification, an act of regeneration followed by growth in grace and increasing mortification of the flesh and the things of the flesh.

The distortions and misunderstandings not only fail to fully understand what the Reformed faith is saying in the perseverance of the saints, but also take away from the glorious work of God in us. For God the Holy Spirit is active in our perseverance as He moves through us and speaks through us. Christ Jesus our Savior prays for us as He prayed for Peter:

> Simon, Simon, behold, Satan demanded to have you, that he might sift you like wheat, but I have prayed for you that your faith may not fail. And when you have turned again, strengthen your brothers. (Luke 22:31–32)

"I have prayed" Jesus says. That is how believers persevere against the devil, the flesh, and the world. But you also persevere "when you have turned again." And then we see that this one who will persevere must feed Christ's sheep by helping them to persevere, for Jesus told Peter to "strengthen your brothers."

Christ keeps us. But we are kept through a holiness created by grace. And we are kept through the ordinary means of grace as we are "strengthened" in the faith in order to strengthen others. What a case for the centrality of the church in our perseverance. This is the impetus behind the admonition from the writer to the Hebrews:

> Let us hold fast the confession of our hope without wavering, for he who promised is faithful. And let

us consider how to stir up one another to love and
good works, not neglecting to meet together, as is
the habit of some, but encouraging one another,
and all the more as you see the Day drawing near.
(Heb. 10:23–25)

And so only those who continue in the faith until the end
shall be saved. And so we must work out our salvation in
fear and trembling.

One of my favorite passages, which I used in planting
two churches and a Christian school, and pastoring a large,
historic downtown church, as well as leading a growing
theological seminary comes from the oldest psalm in the
sacred hymnal of the Bible, Psalm 90, written by Moses:

And let the beauty of the LORD our God be upon us:
and establish thou the work of our hands upon us;
yea, the work of our hands establish thou it. (Ps.
90:17 KJV)

How I want to cling to that Scripture: God must start it.
But He calls on us to respond. But unless He is faithful, all
plans, all hope is for naught. But in Christ our future is
secure "for it is God who works in you, both to will and to
work for his good pleasure" (Phil. 2:13).

THE DEFENSE OF THE DOCTRINE OF PERSEVERANCE

The Reformed doctrine of the perseverance of the
saints does not deny that there are difficult passages. But

having established with so many passages from God's Word that God will keep His flock and not lose any that He chose in love, we admit the "hard" passages, but interpret the "murky" with the clear.

Some have cited the falling away of personages in Scripture. Saul was called to be king of Israel yet forsook the Lord and was finally removed in horrible death, burned up to be found no more. Paul mentions several ministers who served with him, yet fell away, among the most notable was Demas:

> For Demas, in love with this present world, has deserted . . . . (2 Tim. 4:10)

But we could add to this number, the notorious Herod, who heard the preaching of John the Baptist but then sinned openly and even shut off the voice of the prophet by murdering him. And, of course, there was Judas. In this man we have one who was physically close to Jesus, a part of the Twelve, who sat under Jesus' teaching, saw His miracles, witnessed the changed lives, and even saw the dead brought back to life! Yet, Judas betrayed our Lord and died a death of Saul: miserably tragic, horribly violent, and utterly shameful.

The doctrine of the perseverance of the saints, though, does not deny that there are those who make outward professions of faith, but who remain unregenerate. Membership in a visible congregation does not prove membership in the invisible church of Jesus Christ. "Walking the aisle" or "confirmation" or "communicants' classes" or even baptism and taking the Lord's Supper cannot, in themselves, prove that one is saved. The parable of the wheat and the tares proves that. In that teaching of Jesus in Matthew 13,[24] there are some who look like the "real thing" but who are known to God to be what they are: imposters. It was so in my life! I professed faith in Christ, but my life did not show it. It was not until I repented and trusted in Christ alone for eternal life that the Holy Spirit indwelt me, transformed me, and set me on a path of seeking God. And there have been moments of great progress, and times of regrettable and shameful regression. One can have assurance from God's Word that he is saved and safe in the arms of Jesus. One also gains assurance from the testimony of fruit in one's life, loving what God loves and hating what God hates, as well as the witness of the Holy Spirit Himself:

> For you did not receive the spirit of slavery to fall back into fear, but you have received the Spirit of adoption as sons, by whom we cry, "Abba! Father!" (Rom. 8:15)

The doctrine of assurance follows the doctrine of the perseverance of the saints as surely as Christ died for our sins.

But what about the passages in which believers are warned against falling away (e.g., Rom. 11:17–24; 1 Cor. 9:27; Gal. 5:4; Col. 1:23; 1 Thess. 3:5; 1 Tim. 1:19–20; 2 Tim. 2:17–18; James 5:19–20; 2 Peter 2:20–22; 1 John 5:16)? Would there be a warning if in fact God was going to guarantee their salvation? Of course the answer is that the God who *ordains our end* also *ordains the means* to His end

(His purpose for us). And *the means* is obedience flowing from a renewed heart. God calls on believers to be watching in prayer, to watch our own lives, to keep in step with the Holy Spirit, to be baptized, to remember the sacrifice of Jesus Christ in the Lord's Supper, to love one another, to fulfill the Great Commission, and to keep ourselves from idols, just to name a few. But the doctrine of the perseverance of the saints encompasses all of God's means to call us to faithfulness as a way to secure what God intends. I discipline my son because I love him and want him to be kept in my will. And this is what God does. And that is what all of those passages are intended to do in your life and mine.

But what about the famous passage from Hebrews, in which it does seem that there is evidence of one having tasted the things of God, then turning away and, in his sin, "trampling" on the blood of Christ? I speak of Hebrews 6:4–8:

> For it is impossible to restore again to repentance those who have once been enlightened, who have tasted the heavenly gift, and have shared in the Holy Spirit, and have tasted the goodness of the word of God and the powers of the age to come, if they then fall away, since they are crucifying once again the Son of God to their own harm and holding him up to contempt. For land that has drunk the rain that often falls on it, and produces a crop useful to those for whose sake it is cultivated, receives a blessing from God. But if it bears thorns and thistles, it is worthless and near to being cursed, and its end is to be burned.

Here the writer to the Hebrews is speaking of a particular person or group of people who have been so close to Christ, like Judas, and yet have shunned repentance and thus secured a sort of "sin unto death" as John speaks of it, so that their flagrant sin in the presence of the knowledge of Christ is so heinous that it secures their judgment. I like what Matthew Henry says of this to not only explain the text but to comfort fragile consciences that are, in fact, repentant of their sin and desirous of Christ's forgiveness:

> These great things are spoken here of those who may fall away; yet it is not here said of them that they were truly converted, or that they were justified. . . . the apostle describes the dreadful case of such as fall away after having gone so far in the profession of religion.[25]

But Henry assures the sinner who seeks forgiveness that this is not denying him access to Christ no matter what he may have done:

> The humbled sinner who pleads guilty, and cries for mercy, can have no ground from this passage to be discouraged, whatever his conscience may accuse him of. Nor does it prove that any one who is made a new creature in Christ, ever becomes a final apostate from him. . . . If those who through mistaken views of this passage, as well as of their own case, fear that there is no mercy for them, would attend to the account given of the nature of

this sin, that it is a total and a willing renouncing of Christ, and his cause, and joining with his enemies, it would relieve them from wrong fears.[26]

All of the warnings, charges, and admonitions—far from proving that believers may fall away—stir the true believer on to faithfulness to Christ as well as converts the unbeliever for fear of falling under the judgments of almighty God. Thus perseverance is secured for the saint and unrepentant sinners are judged:

> While I was with them, I kept them in your name, which you have given me. I have guarded them, and not one of them has been lost except the son of destruction, that the Scripture might be fulfilled. (John 17:12)

THE DELIGHTS OF THE DOCTRINE OF PERSEVERANCE

The perseverance of the saints, like all of Bible truth, brings blessing for Jesus taught us that truth brings freedom.[27] And doctrine brings delight. Thus for the one who has truly repented and received Jesus Christ as Lord and Savior, he hears Christ say to him:

> Verily, verily, I say unto you, He that heareth my word, and believeth on him that sent me, hath everlasting life, and shall not come into condemnation; but is passed from death unto life. (John 5:24 KJV)

This life in Christ that the believer has is united to Jesus' life. To know that you are now declared righteous before almighty God based on what Jesus Christ has done for you—imputing righteousness to you and taking sin from you through His life and through His death on the cross and resurrection from the dead—is to also be assured that your Savior will never leave you nor forsake you.[28] Indeed, your perseverance is finally secured by the risen Christ interceding for you at the "right hand of the Father":

> Consequently, he is able to save to the uttermost those who draw near to God through him, since he always lives to make intercession for them. (Heb. 7:25)

To know that I am safe in the arms of Jesus forever delights the soul in many ways. Here are only a few:

The perseverance of the saints is a delight to those who are struggling with sin. If you are His and He is yours, dear child of God, the means of grace that Christ has ordained will give you victory. It may be that your struggle lasts your whole life, but can anything withstand the power of the love of Jesus Christ? Nay, "nothing!" says St. Paul. Sin could not finally overcome David. Sin could not finally overcome Peter. The paradox of the gospel is that the very thing that seeks to attack you and destroy you, the very thing which is the source of shame in your life, becomes in the hands of a redeeming God the thing that brings honor to God and good to His children. As the plot of Haman to destroy Esther's people (Est. 3:1–15), and

Mordecai in particular (5:9–14), turned on Haman (8:7)—and he was hung on the gallows built for Mordecai the Jew—so the devil is undone by the very thing he uses to accuse you or shame you. The ruling motif in the believer's life is the cross, the greatest symbol of victory over shame and sin and sorrow and loss. The God who promised that He would restore the years that the locust had eaten (Joel 2:25) is the God who will cause all things—all things—to work together for your good (Rom. 8:28).

The perseverance of the saints is a delight to the believer, for it magnifies the Father who predestined us to salvation in the mystery of His love, as well as Jesus Christ who became the Mediator of this covenant and lived for us and died for us and rose again for us, and the Holy Spirit who actively works in and through us:

> Likewise the Spirit helps us in our weakness. For we do not know what to pray for as we ought, but the Spirit himself intercedes for us with groanings too deep for words. And he who searches hearts knows what is the mind of the Spirit, because the Spirit intercedes for the saints according to the will of God. (Rom. 8:26–27)

This doctrine magnifies God, honors Him, depends upon Him, excites our souls to prayer and adoration, and convinces us of our total dependence upon the Savior.

The perseverance of the saints is a delight to the soul of the saint who needs encouragement to follow the Lord. Far

from engendering lackadaisical attitudes towards sanctification, this doctrine, if received as taught in the Word of
God, promotes holiness of life. For the Scriptures teach
us: "Take care, brothers, lest there be in any of you an evil,
unbelieving heart, leading you to fall away from the living
God" (Heb. 3:12). But the Lord not only warns us so that
we may cling to His grace all the more and then let holy
lives arise from the riches of grace which He has be-
stowed, but He wins us with His promises of persevering
(and I love the language of the old "Authorized Version" at
this point): "He that overcometh . . . shall be clothed in
white raiment; and I will not blot out his name out of the
book of life" (Rev. 3:5 KJV).

The perseverance of the saints is a delight to parents of
prodigals. If your children are Christ's own, then know
that as Christ prayed for Peter, He is praying for your children. No one who has truly, not just tasted, but drank
deep of the grace of God, can stay away from that refreshment forever. I have prayed with many parents whose
children as young adults strayed from the faith. And I have
also watched as those children came home to the Lord.
Sometimes it is not in our time. Sometimes the wait is a
lifetime. But trust in the Lord who teaches us:

> Who shall separate us from the love of Christ? Shall
> tribulation, or distress, or persecution, or famine,
> or nakedness, or danger, or sword? As it is written,
> "For your sake we are being killed all the day long;
> we are regarded as sheep to be slaughtered." No, in
> all these things we are more than conquerors

through him who loved us. For I am sure that neither death nor life, nor angels nor rulers, nor
things present nor things to come, nor powers, nor
height nor depth, nor anything else in all creation,
will be able to separate us from the love of God in
Christ Jesus our Lord. (Rom. 8:35–39)

*The perseverance of the saints is a delight to the souls of
family members who watch their loved ones suffer under the
awful disease of Alzheimer's or other sorts of results of the fall
in this life.* Know that Christ keeps His own even when our
world is darkened by disease and the creation-fallen ef-
fects of aging, for He says, "The hoary head is a crown of
glory, if it be found in the way of righteousness" (Prov.
16:31 KJV) and "even to your old age I am he, and to gray
hairs I will carry you. I have made, and I will bear; I will
carry and will save" (Isa. 46:4).

The perseverance of the saints is a delight to the dying.
The Savior who ordained your salvation before the foundation of the world, who sent His Son to live and die for you
on Calvary's cross, who sent the Spirit to claim you as His
child, will never let you go. And not even the prospect of
death can now shake you from Christ. For it is Christ who
has hold of you. He will keep you safe all the way home:

O death, where is your victory? O death, where is
your sting? (1 Cor. 15:55)

As a pastor I say to you as I have said to the flock of
Jesus in the churches where I have been pastor and to the

students God has given me as a seminary president and professor: "My beloved, always remember—no matter what you are going through, no matter what sin you have committed, no matter what temptations come against you, no matter how hard it is to follow the Lord—that what God starts, God completes."

How eloquently simple were the words of that most pastoral Puritan, Thomas Watson, when he declared:

A Christian's main comfort depends upon this doctrine of perseverance.[29]

SOME CLOSING THOUGHTS

I love this doctrine. It glorifies Jesus Christ just like all of the other doctrines of grace. And it also requires that I bow to the Lord in every part of my salvation. His grace saved me and it is His grace that keeps me. And it will be grace that gets me home.

For those who are inquiring I hope I have given you some helpful Scripture and references to follow up on. Perhaps this little study could also become a starting point for a small group study. Or maybe this time with a friend, with a pastor, has been a time to look again to Jesus Christ. Maybe you are looking to Him for answers to questions about your life. Maybe you are looking to Him because you are at the end of your rope. That is not a bad place to be. It means that you are going to have to start trusting in Christ and Christ alone, not only for your salvation, but for every part of the Christian life. But in the releasing of our death grip on trying to control our lives we are able to take the outreached hand of Christ in this doctrine. And we come to know His grace again.

There is a song that my son and I used to sing together as we headed down Signal Mountain in Tennessee, as I was driving him to school. With our iPod blaring out the clear bluegrass tune from our car speakers, my boy and I would laugh and sing together:

> I'm not holding on to Jesus, He's a holding on to me![30]

And that is the gospel. And that is the perseverance of the saints.

RESOURCES FOR FURTHER STUDY

Berkhof, Louis. *Systematic Theology*. 2d rev. and enl. ed. Grand Rapids: Wm. B. Eerdmans Publishing, 1941.

Boettner, Loraine. *The Reformed Doctrine of Predestination*. Philadelphia: Presbyterian and Reformed, 1965.

Boice, James Montgomery, and Philip Graham Ryken. *The Doctrines of Grace: Rediscovering the Evangelical Gospel*. Wheaton, IL: Crossway Books, 2002.

Cunningham, William. *Historical Theology: A Review of the Principal Doctrinal Discussions in the Christian Church since the Apostolic Age*. 2 vols. Students' Reformed Theological Library. London: Banner of Truth, 1960.

Davis, John Jefferson. "The Perseverance of the Saints: A History of the Doctrine," *Journal of the Evangelical Theological Society* 34, no. 2 (1991): 213–28.

Henry, Matthew. *Commentary on the Whole Bible, Complete and Unabridged in One Volume: Genesis to Revelation*. 17th ed. Peabody, MA: Hendrickson, 1961. Reprint, 2007.

Kelly, Douglas F., Hugh McClure, and Philip B. Rollinson. *The Westminster Confession of Faith: An Authentic Modern Version*. 3rd ed. Signal Mountain, TN: Summertown Texts, 1992.

Kollock, Shepard K. *Perseverance of the Saints: Illustrated, Proved and Applied*. Philadelphia: Presbyterian Tract and Sunday School Society, 1837.

Matthew Henry Commentary. Version 6.0. Accordance Bible Software for Macintosh.

Murray, John. *Redemption, Accomplished and Applied*. Grand Rapids: Wm. B. Eerdmans Publishing, 1955.

Robertson, O. Palmer. *The Christ of the Covenants*. Phillipsburg, NJ: Presbyterian and Reformed, 1980.

Sproul, R. C. *Essential Truths of the Christian Faith*. Wheaton, IL: Tyndale, 1992.

Sproul, R. C., and Keith A. Mathison. *The Reformation Study Bible: English Standard Version*. Orlando, FL: Ligonier Ministries, 2005.

Spurgeon, Charles Haddon. "A Defense of Calvinism." The Spurgeon Archive, [cited January 1, 2008]. Available from http://www. spurgeon.org/calvinis.htm.

Steele, David N., Curtis C. Thomas, and S. Lance Quinn. *The Five Points of Calvinism: Defined, Defended, Documented*. 2nd ed. Phillipsburg, NJ: P&R Publishing, 2004.

Watson, Thomas. *A Body of Divinity: Contained in Sermons upon the Westminster Assembly's Catechism*. Edinburgh: Banner of Truth, 1980. Reprint, 1983.

Williamson, G. I. *The Westminster Confession of Faith: For Study Classes*. 2nd ed. Phillipsburg, NJ: P&R Publishing, 2004.

———. *The Westminster Shorter Catechism: For Study Classes*. 2nd ed. Phillipsburg, NJ: P&R Publishing, 2003.

NOTES

1 See the Prince of Preacher's stouthearted defense of the Reformed faith in Charles Haddon Spurgeon, *A Defense of Calvinism* (The Spurgeon Archive [cited January 1, 2008]), http://www. spurgeon.org/calvinis.htm.

2 Rev. Shepard K. Kollock, *Perseverance of the Saints: Illustrated, Proved and Applied* (Philadelphia: Presbyterian Tract and Sunday School Society, 1837).

3 "But now thus says the LORD, he who created you, O Jacob, he who formed you, O Israel: 'Fear not, for I have redeemed you; I have called you by name, you are mine'" (Isa. 43:1).

4 Buddy Green, "River of Refreshment," from the compact disc *Hymns and Prayer Songs*, Spring Hill, 2005.

5 In the "Great Eighth"—the eighth chapter of Paul's Epistle to the Romans—the apostle vigorously advances the doctrine of the perseverance of the saints as he preaches with his pen: "Who will bring any charge against those whom God has chosen? It is God who justifies. Who is he that condemns? Christ Jesus, who died—more than that, who was raised to life—is at the right hand of God and is also interceding for us. Who shall separate us from the love

of Christ? Shall trouble or hardship or persecution or famine or nakedness or danger or sword? As it is written: 'For your sake we face death all day long; we are considered as sheep to be slaughtered.' No, in all these things we are more than conquerors through him who loved us. For I am convinced that neither death nor life, neither angels nor demons, neither the present nor the future, nor any powers, neither height nor depth, nor anything else in all creation, will be able to separate us from the love of God that is in Christ Jesus our Lord" (Rom. 8:33–39 NIV).

6   For example, Jesus prayed: "I will remain in the world no longer, but they are still in the world, and I am coming to you. Holy Father, protect them by the power of your name—the name you gave me—so that they may be one as we are one" (John 17:11 NIV). See the implicit understanding that the Father will protect and preserve all believers in Jesus so that God's plan of the ages may be realized.

7   Are there any more beautiful promises about the perseverance of the saints than in Jeremiah, as the people of God are facing judgment? Consider only these two wonderful passages and ask yourself, "Can a man be truly saved of the Lord and yet be lost by God?" "The LORD appeared to us in the past, saying: "I have loved you with an everlasting love; I have drawn you with loving-kindness" (Jer. 31:3 NIV); and "I will make an everlasting covenant with them: I will never stop doing good to them, and I will inspire them to fear me, so that they will never turn away from me" (Jer. 32:40 NIV). What grace is shown in the keeping power of God to those about to go through trials and even judgment! Yet nothing can separate them from the love of God. And God's love itself will "inspire them."

8   David was chosen of the Lord. Yet his sin distanced him from God. But the testimony of the sweet singer of Israel was this: "For day and night your hand was heavy upon me; my strength was sapped as in the heat of summer. *Selah*" (Ps. 32:4 NIV). Even in his spiritual distance from God, God was not distant from him. David, through God, persevered in his relationship to God, for God had

established the relationship Himself. Or consider how David was kept by God as his enemies encamped around him, as in Psalm 34: "The angel of the LORD encamps around those who fear him, and delivers them" (Ps. 34:7). God deploys heavenly beings to purposely keep the saints. God employs mortal men and "ordinary" circumstances to providentially preserve His people.

9 We have seen the famous Good Shepherd passage from John 10, but consider the beauty of these passages and how they, too, teach that what God starts, God completes: "Truly, truly, I say to you, whoever hears my word and believes him who sent me has eternal life. He does not come into judgment, but has passed from death to life" (John 5:24); and "I am the living bread that came down from heaven. If anyone eats of this bread, he will live forever. And the bread that I will give for the life of the world is my flesh" (John 6:51).

10 John Murray, *Redemption, Accomplished and Applied* (Grand Rapids: Wm. B. Eerdmans Publishing, 1955).

11 William Cunningham, *Historical Theology: A Review of the Principal Doctrinal Discussions in the Christian Church since the Apostolic Age*, 2 vols., Students' Reformed Theological Library (London: Banner of Truth Trust, 1960).

12 Loraine Boettner, *The Reformed Doctrine of Predestination* (Philadelphia: Presbyterian and Reformed Publishing, 1965). Citation is taken from *Accordance* Bible software, Version 7.0.

13 Augustine, *Treatise on the Gift of Perseverance*, as quoted in John Jefferson Davis, "The Perseverance of the Saints: A History of the Doctrine," *Journal of the Evangelical Theological Society* 34, no. 2 (1991).

14 Ibid.

15 For a brief review of this and other basic Bible truths, see R. C. Sproul, *Essential Truths of the Christian Faith* (Wheaton, IL: Tyndale, 1992). For a deeper study of "covenant" in particular, see O. Palmer Robertson, *The Christ of the Covenants* (Phillipsburg, NJ: Presbyterian and Reformed, 1980).

16 Robertson, *The Christ of the Covenants*, 4.

17 The five points of Calvinism are, in fact, not the whole teaching of John Calvin on theology or his major views on the Reformed faith. They are, in fact, direct answers, put in an acrostic for English speakers, to the five specific "remonstrances" (protests) of the followers of a Dutch theologian named James Arminius. The protest was made by the "Arminians" as this group came to be called, in 1610. The response to this charge was studiously provided by 84 pastors and theologians and 18 representatives of the Dutch government. After 154 sessions, lasting from 1618–19 (called "The Synod of Dordt" for the meetings were held in the Dutch town of Dordt), this stalwart band of believers produced what became known as "The Five Points of Calvinism." For a study of this, in particular, I would recommend two books: James Montgomery Boice and Philip Graham Ryken, *The Doctrines of Grace: Rediscovering the Evangelical Gospel* (Wheaton, IL: Crossway Books, 2002), and David N. Steele, Curtis C. Thomas, and S. Lance Quinn, *The Five Points of Calvinism: Defined, Defended, Documented*, 2nd ed. (Phillipsburg, NJ: P&R Publishing, 2004).

18 Louis Berkhof, *Systematic Theology*, 2nd rev. and enl. ed. (Grand Rapids: Wm. B. Eerdmans Publishing, 1941), 541.

19 For a good modern English translation, faithfully preserving the doctrinal integrity of the original, see Douglas F. Kelly, Hugh McClure, and Philip B. Rollinson, *The Westminster Confession of Faith: An Authentic Modern Version*, 3rd ed. (Signal Mountain, TN: Summertown Texts, 1992), G. I. Williamson, *The Westminster Confession of Faith: For Study Classes*, 2nd ed. (Phillipsburg, NJ: P&R Publishing, 2004).

20 It has been said, with a smile, that Methodists teach like Arminians but compose hymns like Calvinists!

21 Fanny Crosby, "Safe in the Arms of Jesus," 1868.

22 The Westminster Shorter Catechism remains the preeminent study for learning about basic Bible truths. Consider the succinct definition of "sanctification:" "Q. 35. What is sanctification? A. Sanctification is the work of God's free grace, whereby we are renewed in the whole man after the image of God, and are enabled

more and more to die unto sin, and live unto righteousness." See G. I. Williamson, *The Westminster Shorter Catechism: For Study Classes*, 2nd ed. (Phillipsburg, NJ: P&R Publishing, 2003).

23 "Therefore, my beloved, as you have always obeyed, so now, not only as in my presence but much more in my absence, work out your own salvation with fear and trembling" (Phil. 2:12).

24 "He put another parable before them, saying, 'The kingdom of heaven may be compared to a man who sowed good seed in his field, but while his men were sleeping, his enemy came and sowed weeds among the wheat and went away. So when the plants came up and bore grain, then the weeds appeared also. And the servants of the master of the house came and said to him, "Master, did you not sow good seed in your field? How then does it have weeds?" He said to them, "An enemy has done this." So the servants said to him, "Then do you want us to go and gather them?" But he said, "No, lest in gathering the weeds you root up the wheat along with them. Let both grow together until the harvest, and at harvest time I will tell the reapers, Gather the weeds first and bind them in bundles to be burned, but gather the wheat into my barn." ' " (Matt. 13:24–30); "Then he left the crowds and went into the house. And his disciples came to him, saying, 'Explain to us the parable of the weeds of the field.' He answered, 'The one who sows the good seed is the Son of Man. The field is the world, and the good seed is the children of the kingdom. The weeds are the sons of the evil one, and the enemy who sowed them is the devil. The harvest is the close of the age, and the reapers are angels. Just as the weeds are gathered and burned with fire, so will it be at the close of the age. The Son of Man will send his angels, and they will gather out of his kingdom all causes of sin and all law-breakers, and throw them into the fiery furnace. In that place there will be weeping and gnashing of teeth. Then the righteous will shine like the sun in the kingdom of their Father. He who has ears, let him hear.' " (Matt. 13:36–43).

25 Matthew Henry, *Commentary on the Whole Bible, Complete and Unabridged in One Volume: Genesis to Revelation*, 17th ed. (Peabody, MA: Hendrickson Publishers, 1961; reprint, 2007).

26 Matthew Henry Commentary, Version 6.0, Accordance Bible Software for Macintosh.

27 "And you will know the truth, and the truth will set you free" (John 8:32).

28 "Be strong and courageous. Do not fear or be in dread of them, for it is the LORD your God who goes with you. He will not leave you or forsake you" (Deut. 31:6); [and] ". . . for he has said, 'I will never leave you nor forsake you' " (Heb. 13:5).

29 Thomas Watson, *A Body of Divinity: Contained in Sermons upon the Westminster Assembly's Catechism* (Edinburgh: Banner of Truth, 1983), 279.

30 Ron Block, "He's Holding on to Me," *Faraway Land* compact disc recording, release date August 7, 2001. © Ron Block 2001.